Be Healed!

How to Unlock the Supernatural Healing Power of God

by Robert Rite

Table of Contents

Get Complimentary Access to: "Prophecy Alerts"

Dear reader: Prophecies are being fulfilled so rapidly in these last days that I am offering my readers complimentary access to "*prophecy alerts*" so that you get "*Breaking Prophecy News*" as soon as it breaks...Just follow this link below and sign Up today...
http://robertritebooks.com/prophecy-alerts/

Disclaimer:

This book in no way offers any medical advice. The reader should consult a medical professional regarding any health matters.   Any illness or disease must be consulted with and treated by a licensed physician, hospital and/or clinic. God who created everything, also created medical professionals, clinics and hospitals for a divine purpose!

Chapter 1 - The Good News

Mark 5:34 And He said to her, "Daughter, your faith has made you well. Go in peace, and be healed of your affliction."

There are about 17 spiritual gifts that God bestows upon us. Each of us (whether a believer or not) is born with one or more of these gifts. Many never even realize that they have a spiritual gift and so the gift is wasted. But God wants us to discover and to cultivate these gifts so that we can glorify the Lord during our time here on earth.

God provides much more than just physical healing. God provides spiritual and emotional healing as well. God heals those who suffer and are heartbroken. God can heal marriages, loneliness, addictions, depression, hatred, poverty, and any other affliction. God can heal us from anything. In this book I will try to stay focused on just one of these spiritual gifts - the gift of healing.

So what is the good news? It is about how we can all be healed of our afflictions, and that we can all live a longer, happier and more productive life. The good news is that no matter how bad things get out there, and what we witness when we watch the morning or evening news, you can still find peace in this life.

After reading this book you will better understand that when you operate within the kingdom of God, you can receive kingdom power and then nothing inside of our dimension becomes impossible.

When Jesus was here on earth he spent most his time preaching the good news (the Gospels). What is this good news? It is that after his death, the gift of the Holy Spirit would avail itself to anyone who asked for it in the name of the Lord. This supernatural spirit equips us to overcome all temptations, fears and worries, most of life's tragedies, illnesses, among other blessings. The Holy Spirit is our enabler our helper. John 14:16 "And I will pray the Father, and He will give you another Helper, that He may abide with you forever"

What Jesus did thousands of years ago when he healed hundreds of people, was his example to us. Through his spirit in us, we can manifest the power to heal and to perform the good works that the Lord demonstrated for us. Although he is no longer walking on the earth, the Lord still manifests his healing power for us, and through us!

When we accept the Messiah as our Lord and savior we are empowered to receive the Holy Spirit. The gift of the Holy Spirit is the heavenly force that releases in us a spiritual and supernatural power to rebuke all illness and pain from our bodies and the bodies of our loved ones. Since we are to love our neighbors as ourselves we should openly offer this power (gift) of healing to our fellow man.

God expects to manifest himself in us. But he will only do that if we allow him in (and we should since he created us and our body belongs to him). All we need is to have the confidence and faith to claim healing and to release all illnesses in Jesus name.

There are so many souls out there who need healing. Some are in great physical pain; others need emotional healing. As the salt of the earth, we can reach out to heaven and release power to heal their pain.

Why Does God Allow Sickness into our Lives?

Sickness is a consequence of original sin – prior to that there was no sickness. God does not want us to be sick. Jesus died to allow us to be healed physically and spiritually. But sometimes healing does not come this side of heaven. Healing comes in different ways such as dipping in water, mud in eyes, by a shadow, by intersession James 5:14-15, via handkerchiefs; anointing in oil, and healing can occur all in Gods time and manner.

We should pray persistently and bind the power of the spirit of sickness and disease. You see, God gets glory when we prosper in health and in all areas of life. The word reveals that by his stripes we are healed.

Now let's explore what God's supernatural power of healing can do for and through us.

Chapter 2 - God's Promises for Healing

Luke 9:7; "Then he called his 12 disciples together, and gave them the power and authority over all devils and to cure disease.

The bible is full of promises and examples of healing. Before departing, Jesus in fact commanded his disciples (this includes you and I if we are his followers) to heal the sick. We were given the awesome and distinguished honor to carry his torch; his message of good news and his miracles to the world.

We were also given the mandate, and with the mandate came the power to heal the sick (and ourselves of course)! Let's review some of these promises:

Genesis 20:17 Abraham prayed and God healed Abimilek. We learn here that Abraham did not have the gift of healing but he prayed for healing!

Proverbs 4:20-22 Teaches us that we can be healed by reading the word of God: "My son, pay attention to what I say; turn your ear to my words. Do not let them out of your sight; keep them within your heart; for they are life to those who find them and health (healing) to one's whole body."

Exodus 23:25 God will remove sickness from those who worship him.

Jeremiah 30:17 God promises to restore us to health and to heal our wounds. Please remember that although these promises were to Israel in this example – they pertain to all who read and embrace these words from God!

Proverbs Ch. 4 vs. 20-22: "My son, give attention to my words; Incline your ear to my sayings. Do not let them depart from your eyes; Keep them in the midst of your heart; for they are life to those who find them, and health to all their flesh.

Psalm 107:20 "He sent His word and healed them, and delivered them from their destructions (healing comes from the word)"

Isaiah 53:4-5 We are healed by Jesus death at the cross. "By his stripes we are healed."

Mathew 18:18: "Assuredly, I say to you, whatever you bind on earth will be bound in heaven, and whatever you loose on earth will be loosed in heaven."

Luke 9:1-2 "When Jesus had called the Twelve together, he gave them power and authority to drive out all demons and to cure diseases, and he sent them out to proclaim the kingdom of God and to heal the sick.

Luke 9:7; "Then he called his 12 disciples together, and gave them the power and authority over all devils and to cure disease."

Luke 10:19 teaches us that God's promises go beyond just physical healing:"Behold I give unto you power to tread on serpents and scorpions, and over all the power of the enemy, and nothing shall by any means hurt you".
The above are just a few of the promises of healing found in the bible. So it is apparent from this that God wanted to make it clear to us that we have the power to heal the sick, among other things, if we choose to and learn how to harness that supernatural power.

More Bible Versus on Healing

- **Jeremiah 17:14**

- **James 5:16 confess our sins first**

- **2 Corinthians 1:20**

- **James 5:14-15**

- **Romans 8:11**

- **Mark 16:18**

- **Jeremiah 32:27**

- **Exodus 23:25-26**

- **Psalm 21:4; Psalm 42:11; Psalm 103:2-3**

- **Jeremiah 30:17**

- **Proverbs 4:20-22**

- **2 Chronicles 20:22**

- **Exodus 15:26**

- **Numbers 23:19**

- **Deuteronomy 5:33 and 7:11-15 and 30:19-20**

- **2 Chronicles 16:9; 30:20**

- **Job 37:23**

- Psalm 32; 34:19; 41:3; 91:10-16; 103:2-3; 105:37; 107:20; 147:3

- Proverbs 3:1-2; Proverbs 3:7-8; 4:20-22; 9:11; 14:30; 16:24

- Isaiah 40:29; 40:31; 41:10; 53:4-5; 55:11; 58:8

- Jeremiah 17:14; 30:17

– Malachi 3:6; 4:2

- Mathew 4:23-24; 7:11; 8:2-3; 8:5-13; 8:14-17; 9:20-22; 9:27-35; 10:1; 10:7-8; 11:2-5; 12:15; 14:13-14; 14:34-36 — 15:29-31; 18:19-20; 19:1-2; 21:14; 24:35

- Mark 1:32-34; 2:1-12; 5:21-43; 6:5-6; 6:53-56; 10:46-52; 11:23-24; 16:15-20

- Luke 4:16-21 — 4:40 — 6:6-10 — 7:11-16 — 9:1-2, 6-11 — 10:8-9

- John 5:2-14 — 9:1-7 — 10:10 — 14:13-14 — 15:7 — 16:23-24

- Acts 3:1-8 — 5:12 — 5:16 — 8:5-8 — 9:33-34 — 10:38 — 14:8-10 — 19:11-12

- Romans 4:19-21; Romans 8-11; Romans 8:32

- 1 Corinthians 6:20; 12:7-11; 28

- Ephesians 6:1-3

- 1 Thessalonians 5:23-24

- Hebrews 4:14-16; 10:23; 10:35-36; 11:1; 11:6; 13:8

- James 1:17; 5:14-16

- 1 peter 2:24

- 1 John 5:14-15

- 3 John 1:2

Can Our Life be extended beyond what God has planned for us?

I have more good news for those of you who have missed opportunities in life due to protracted illnesses.

God can not only restore your health, he can also restore back time for you that may have been lost due to illness. Of course this requires great faith on your part. Also when God says it is time to go home - it is time! That said God can do whatever he wants because God is God!

In the book of Isaiah Chapter 38:1-we learn that King Hezekiah, who had much faith on the Lord, fell sick and Isaiah received a message from God to tell King Hezekiah to get his house in order because he was going to die and was not going to recover from that illness. Well Hezekiah despite this certain message of death from both God and the great prophet Isaiah, he prayed and wept bitterly for healing Isaiah 38:2-3. God heard his prayer, and commanded Isaiah to tell King Hezekiah the following: "….I have heard your prayer and seen your tears, I will add 15 years to your life." God also defended his city which was being attacked by the Assyrians. Isaiah 38:4-6

Also, in the book of Joel 2:25 God teaches that he can "repay you for the years the locusts have eaten…."   Here again we see how God restores time lost due to illnesses or any other trials of life!

So do not be shy in asking the Lord for anything, especially when it comes to miraculous healing. God is not restricted by time, or by anything else. So the measure of what God grants us or blesses us with in our life is usually tied to the measure of what we ask for in faith.

Chapter 3 - Basic Requirements for receiving Supernatural Healing

Acts 14:9...This man heard Paul speaking. Paul, observing him intently and seeing that he had faith to be healed

Let's review some basic requirements that we need before we can manifest the gift of healing in our life.

Nothing good comes easy and without any effort on our part. To receive the awesome power to heal and be healed, there are a few things we need to equip ourselves with. These include:

1) Faith - Claim God's will and promises of healing, believe with faith.

2) Prayer (pray regularly)

3) The word - Stay immersed in the word of God (24/7). Stay focused on the word. Occupy your mind with the healing not the symptoms! Proverbs 4 vs. 20-22

4) Make sure that there is no un-forgiveness in your heart (pray: "Lord I forgive everybody including myself")

5) make sure that there is no ongoing sin in your life (that you have

repented of past and present sin, and that you are committing to put an end to this sin, or sins. Reconcile with God, ask for forgiveness of all sin in your life – consecrate yourself in preparation for healing.

Have others pray with and For You

Have your family, friends and church members pray for your healing. Even if you have no family or friends, in his mercy, God still provides for you! There are many Christian help lines throughout the world that you can call, and they will pray with you for your healing.

What to do when someone is praying for you in person or over the phone
When someone is praying or laying hands on you in person or over the phone there are three things that you should (or not do):

1) Clear your mind - do not pray while your healer is praying for you - just listen and focus on the words with total faith (you can't transmit and receive at same time)

2) Don't try to get healed. When you are desperately trying or are fearful that you may not receive healing - then you are getting in the way of receiving the healing.

3) Just relax and receive.

Chapter 4 - Examples of Supernatural healing

Luke 5:15 However, the report went around concerning Him all the more; and great multitudes came together to hear, and to be healed by Him of their infirmities

Some people believe that the gift of healing ended with Jesus Christ and that miracles no longer happen. Nothing can be further from the truth! Below are just a few examples of many witnessed healings....

Chad Dedmon (Christian pastor) - As a youth Chad had a rebellious spirit and got involved in drugs and alcohol. While in his lost state he started having demonic visions. Then one day he had a vision and he could see Jesus reaching to him weeping. Jesus gave him ultimatum "be my best friend or be handed over to Satan"! He wisely chose Jesus! As soon as he committed his life to the Lord - the desire for drugs instantly left him."

Now years later as a strong Christian and minister he prayed for a man born blind from birth. He was born with no eyeballs. Upon laying hands on this man, they were formed instantly. Now get this - the man's eyes were initially blue and he could not see perfectly. But gradually his eye color changed to brown and he could then see perfectly.

Did you know that babies sometimes are born with baby blue eyes and cannot see clearly at first but when their eyes mature to their natural color - they then can see clearly? So God gave this blind man the brand new eyes that he was born without! Brand new eyes, right out of the box! Is God awesome or what! In another case, a woman who could not hear was given new perfect hearing.

Kevin Dedman In his book unlocking heaven, Kevin writes of experiences he has had while healing others. A drug addict and an alcoholic were totally healed.

Tony Kemp (author) states that "the Presence and Power of the Lord is here; when you receive a revelation of the word, and you respond to revelation (word of knowledge), then you will release a supernatural manifestation of healing for either yourself or others.

John Fenn (Christian minister): claims that the Lord revealed to him that he could have his spiritual senses activated, that he could see into the supernatural. After this revelation, for 2 weeks straight anyone he touched was healed.

Nick Griemsmann's story. In chapter 6, you can read the moving story of a person who struggled from severe mental illness.

Note: The bible does reveal that we can see into the supernatural realm.
In **2 Kings 6:17** we read how Elijah asked God to open his servant's eye so he could see what Elijah saw (a vast invisible army of God's soldiers ready to defend them). As Jesus taught us, nothing is impossible when we operate in perfect faith.

Chapter 5 - How to Pray for Supernatural Healing

Hebrews 12:13...and make straight paths for your feet, so that what is lame may not be dislocated, but rather be healed.

Prayer is very powerful because the spoken word is very powerful. Words can be spoken

for the good or for bad. In this book we will focus on words for the good.

We will all encounter disease and illnesses in our life. Below are some powerful prayers that you can use to pray for yourself or others.....

General Illness:

"In the name of Jesus, I take authority over this sickness and disease and I command it to leave from my (or the other person's) body now - be healed in the name of Jesus"

You can also pray this for any illness as follows...

"In the name of Jesus, I speak to the demonic power giving life to (name the illness) in (or name of person's) body, I call you out, and I command the pain and the reason for the pain in Jesus name to leave this body right NOW. Be healed in Jesus name".

You can pray for any affliction, for example for weight loss, you may pray as follows...

"Father let the angels of healing take their position, Father I release your power of kingdom healing. I know that power comes out of your glory. I hereby command the miracle of supernatural weight loss into my (or the person's name) in Jesus name for your glory, amen"

For multiple afflictions, you can continue as follows:

..."I further speak for a miracle of healing of this (name the illness) for (your or the person's name) to be healed right now in the name of Jesus"

For supposed irreparable illness (such as missing limbs, slipped disks, Scoliosis, or whatever), you can pray as follows....

"In the name of Jesus I suspend time, I command this (name the infirmity) to disappear, I call from the 3rd heaven a brand new (name the organ or whatever is damaged or missing), let it be put in your/his/her body now. I command the spirit of pain and the reason for the pain to be healed right now. I command all side effects thereof to leave right now in Jesus name, amen."

We can even pray for improved finances and wealth:

"Lord God in the name of Jesus I believe your word that Jesus was made poor so that we may be made rich, he has completed his work, and I receive that completed work, I declare by the word of God that I am made rich. I receive an anointing for wealth and a war chest and in the name of Jesus the Angels are released to go and bind the spirits of poverty, to plunder the servants of evil and bring me their spoils. I am a tither and a giver and as a result I'm

18

full of wealth, it comes to me now in the name of Jesus."

Other sample prayers:

"Heavenly father, in the name of Jesus and in the power of that name; let your anointing flow through my hands. I declare by the stripes of Jesus that I have received healing in Jesus Holy name, by my faith in the name and in his blood, I claim and receive your healing right now".   Now confidently repeat (as many times as you wish): "The power of God is working inside of me, and I thank God that I have received healing."

David and Barbara Cerullo (fellow Christian ministers and authors) offer the following prayer for healing. You can replace the spaces provide below with your name or the name(s) of the person(s) you are praying for....

"Father we come before you today in the name of Jesus – we thank you Lord Jesus that you paid the price for our healing and that by your stripes we are healed – we thank you Father that we have the right to come before you and to appropriate your healing power in _____ life. We know Lord you get no honor from the sickness or poverty of your children, but that you get honor when your children are blessed and prospering and healthy because it reveals to the world your glory and your power and your righteousness, and what a great Father we serve. So Father we come before you now and in the name of Jesus we rebuke any spirit of disease and sickness that has afflicted _____. We rebuke every work of the curse that would come against _____ mind, body and against _____ spirit.

Every spirit of infirmity, we command you Satan and spirits of sickness of disease not in our name but in the name of Jesus Christ, and in the authority of the word of God, we command your spirits of disease to be released from _____ body NOW -
Father in the heavens we ask that you bind the powers and principalities of the enemy and rebuke the enemy that comes against _____ with sickness and disease in the heavens for you

said that you will bind in heaven what we bind in earth and you would lose in heaven what we lose on earth. So Father right now we speak healing over_____ we say to you now by the stripes of Jesus _____ is healed.
Right now let the healing virtue of Jesus Christ flow through _____ body and make _____ 100% whole in Jesus name – be healed in the name of Jesus.

Father in the heavens we ask you to release your spirit of healing – let your ministering angels go right now and minister healing to _____. To their body, mind emotions, spirit. Minister your healing to their family and broken relationships and every area of their life. In the name of Jesus, I thank and praise you and bless your name because you are God almighty and there is none other – and your power can conquer all. We thank you God the Almighty in the name of Jesus of Nazareth, AMEN!!!!

NOTE: You should pray in your own words following the above outline. Your own style for communicating to the Creator is precious to his ears! God gave us each our own unique spirit so he will listen to us when we speak from our heart! The key is that you pray in faith and in expectation to receive an answer.

In closing out this chapter, let me pray for you...

"Heavenly father God, I pray for all those souls that are currently enduring pain, suffering and illness in their life. I pray that the healing power of the Holy Spirit and the sanctified blood of Jesus manifest itself in them and heal them right now. I pray that all who believe, that by their faith they are quickly healed; that through their healing they may serve as a witness to those whom they encounter throughout their life. I pray that those that they heal may also harness your kingdom power; so that this healing miracle spreads like an uncontrollable virus and heal millions more. We thank you Lord as we witness your healing in our lives and in the lives of our loved ones; we worship your glory Lord and glorify almighty God in heaven, Amen"

Chapter 6 - Be Healed from Depression and Mental Illness

Mark 5:23 ...and he begged Him earnestly, saying, "My little daughter lies at the point of death. Come and lay your hands on her, that she may be healed, and she will live."

I wanted to include a section on healing depression and mental illness because it is such a widespread illness throughout America and the world. It is particularly prevalent among the teenage and young adults today. The complexities and challenges of today's society and high demands it places on us is one of the major contributors to this disease.

Depression is a debilitating illness, and many people suffer from different forms of depression. It is an epidemic in society that causes feelings of deep sadness, emptiness, apathy and or distorted thinking. Conservatively, 1 in 10 persons suffer from depression. 1 out of 4 women and 1 out of 8 men suffer from this illness. It is twice as common in women as in men. It has been reported that 1 in 3 people that an internal medicine physician sees is suffering from clinical depression.

In fact, Dr. Nedley (Founder of Nedley Health Solutions) believes that in the younger generation 1 in 2 may be suffering from depression. Many have it and have not sought help, perhaps not aware they have it, or thinking that it is a normal process they are going through.

Depression does not discriminate from the rich or the poor, man or women – it affects all types of good folks, including Christians.

The bible provides many inferences of depression with words such as sorrow, anxiety, suffering, being troubled, worry, afraid, and related terms. Satan attacks our mind in an effort to distort our thinking and that is why I believe that depression is so common especially in these last days that we

live in.

Elijah Suffered From Depression

In the bible we learn that Elijah suffered from depression, and how Angels had to help get him out of his depressed state. They had to feed him, and wake him out of his depressed state (Read **1 Kings 19:4-15**). The episode begins in 1 kings 4: "while he himself went a day's journey into the wilderness. He came to a broom bush, sat down under it and prayed that he might die. "I have had enough, Lord," he said. "Take my life; I am no better than my ancestors." 5 Then he lay down under the bush and fell asleep.

King Solomon Suffered From Depression

Solomon who had been blessed with enormous wisdom and wealth suffered from a need to desire all of the pleasures that he could imagine. He tried it all; anything that gave Solomon pleasure he had to do it, even getting involved in his wives' idol worshiping. As a result – his relationship with God was compromised, and this all led him to depression. We learn in Ecclesiastes that despite all of his wealth and power, in the end he hated his life. Read Ecclesiastes 1 and also: Ecclesiastes 2:17 – "So I hated life, because the work that is done under the sun was grievous to me.

All of it is meaningless, a chasing after the wind."

Also the first anointed King of Israel - King Saul suffered from depression, but in his case he did not deal with it properly (**Read 1 Samuel, and 1 Samuel 28:5-20**). Self inflated pride sometimes leads to wounded pride which could lead to depression. This is precisely what led to King Saul's demise, and also the death of King Nebuchadnezzar.

Can Depression and Mental Illness be healed?

Nick Griemsmann lost his parents at the age of 8. By 10 he was already addicted to pornography. By age 21 he was a drug addict and alcoholic with suicidal thoughts. Soon thereafter he was diagnosed with full blown Schizophrenia. One day he received a brochure from a local church. He attended the church and he asked that they pray for him. When they prayed he felt better - but not healed.

He became immersed in the word, listened to gospel music and praying with confidence of healing - rebuking the spirit of mental illness. One day he felt this restraining force leave his body. What was left was this enormous feeling of peace and from that they forward he became completely healed. Today he is an author and a minister for those suffering from his illness. And if that were not enough, he is now the administrator at the same institution that he was a patient at - managing a staff of 50!

There is no illness, disease, sickness or deformity out there that cannot be healed, given the appropriate measure of faith. To believe that God cannot heal a certain type of illness simply demonstrates a low level of faith, and it questions God's Omniscience and omnipotence.

Chapter 7 - Why you might not be receiving Healing even after much Prayer

James 5:16...Confess your trespasses to one another, and pray for one another, that you may be healed. The effective, fervent prayer of a righteous man avails much.

Okay, so some of you may have prayed and may have felt or received nothing. Well I'll be!
First, we must understand that God does NOT operate in our dimension of time. God operates outside of the limits of time. He occupies and he controls all dimensions. Including dimensions that our mortal bodies and mind are not capable of comprehending.

God delays healing sometimes because he needs us to first straighten out our spiritual life. He may also be trying to get our attention, or to strengthen our faith, character or spiritual fortitude. God may be testing our faith, by making us wait for our healing. Perhaps God is arranging to put us in touch with someone empowered with the gift of healing.

We all like to have control over our life and our daily matters. And we know that we are all limited by time. As a result, many become impatient when something happens that restricts their ability to move forward; to progress in life. So when a problem arrives that they can't fix, and that requires God's help, many want immediate solution from God (kind of like what little babies do when they want something).   This itself may block them from getting an answer. They fail to accept that God is not our servant and that he does not answer to our schedule.

Many people have lost faith because God perhaps did not or has not answered a prayer. They have perhaps endured an affliction for many years. Again, please recognize that God does not operate in our dimension of time. Many times the miracle may be delayed indefinitely due to our lack of faith. Sometimes it may be because of sin in our life. And other times it is because God is testing our enduring faith! Be patient and have faith - you shall be rewarded - Guaranteed. But it will be in God's time.

Indeed, one of the main reason many do not receive healing is because they do not have faith. We must claim God's will and promise of healing, and believe with faith, and then we can be healed! It may not be today or tomorrow, but because of your faith - in God's timing...you will receive healing! After all what is faith? Faith is all about waiting on God for our needs, such as healing.

Some people are healed instantly and others are not. For some it is because of their level of faith (or lack thereof), and for others it is because of God's grace (and not because they deserve it) that they receive their miracle. Many times it is because God is refining our level of faith, molding us into the person he wants us to become, and trying to get our attention and our focus on him instead of the things of this world.

Sometimes during a period of protracted illness we draw closer to God by prayer and reading his word. Sadly for many, they never reach out to God except when they need healing or some other thing from God....as if God is there servant – role reversal at its worst!

If you expect to receive an answer solution to an illness, a problem, or whatever it is that you are praying for - then you may indeed be disappointed. God rewards faith and perseverance. Sometimes you may be healed instantly, while other times it endures for years as a test of your faith.

But remember this, the faithful will ALWAYS be rewarded; either in this life, or the life thereafter. Even if the pain persists all of our life, those who remain faithful and endure to the end, these are the ones who are guaranteed an eternity of joy and peace void of all pain and suffering in a place so divine that our mortal bodies are incapable of comprehending it. In heaven we will have supernatural senses designed to fully take in and enjoy the whole glory of God Almighty. It will be a reward well worth the wait!

We read in Genesis 21 how Abraham would finally bear a child (Isaac) through Sarah, after having to wait 40 years for this promise to manifest itself. By then Abraham was 100 years old and Sarah around 90! Impossible right? Well nothing is impossible to God. Because of Abraham's faith all the nations and all the people of the earth have been blessed. It is through the line of Isaac that the Messiah Yeshua (Jesus) was born, and through his death the redemption of sin was made available to all mankind so that we ALL have the ability to become children of God.

Here are some other reasons we may not be receiving our promise of healing:

1) Insufficient knowledge of the healing power of the Gospel; the word of God.

2) Lack of prayer time and united prayer (it is fine to pray alone, but the more people with faith that you have praying for you, the better your chances for healing). Go to a healing meeting - there is power in numbers, and this also applies to prayer power.

3) Traditions and misperceptions of mankind (such as those who believe that "sickness is the will of God", or "the age of miracles has past", or "it's not God's will to heal all")

4) When we break natural laws. When we abuse our body (smoking, drinking, take drugs, eat unhealthy, etc.).

5) When we lack faith in God's healing power.

6) When we have unresolved sin and un-forgiveness in your heart/life.

7) When we are not immersed in the word. The more we read, the more we learn, and knowledge is power.

8) When we harbor any un-forgiveness in our life.

9) When we are living is sin. This is one of the main reasons for un-answered prayer. Consecrate yourself in preparation for healing.

In **Mathew 13:57-58** we learn that Jesus did not heal some because of their lack of faith. And in **Mark 6:4-6** we learn that when a person or community does not have faith, he/they cannot be healed by God: "Jesus said to them, "A prophet is not without honor except in his own town, among his relatives and in his own home." He could not do any miracles there, except lay his hands on a few sick people and healing them. He was amazed at their lack of faith."

So don't stop praying, don't lose hope. Just be patient and confident in your faith. When you live in faith, your promise of healing may manifest itself at any time.

Should we seek medical help or advice, or would this compromise our supernatural healing?

Of course we should seek medical help when we suffer from chronic illness or disease. Who created medicine? Man did not create doctors or medicines, God did! And out of God's love and mercy, he blessed and enabled many good people to create and invent healing medicines and procedures! The problem is that many people do not want to give credit to God for anything. Yet when they get sick or ill, many immediate reject God because of their suffering and blame him for all of their ills!

There is no reason to NOT seek medical attention whenever we need healing. After All God uses Doctors and hospitals as instruments of physical healing for both those with and those without faith. But it cannot hurt to add faith into the healing picture – it is like the icing on the cake!

But while we are receiving medical attention, it can only help expedite the entire healing process if we immerse ourselves in prayer for rapid healing. This faith in spiritual healing will perhaps make the medication work even better and faster for you! It is like the icing on the cake of healing, if you will!

But for heaven's sake (pardon the pun here), do not place your faith and trust in your doctor, your clinic or your meds. Keep your faith and your trust where it belongs on the God who created your doctors, your clinic and your meds!

Chapter 8 - Why faith is so Important

Luke 7:7
therefore I did not even think myself worthy to come to you. But say the word, and my servant will be healed

By now you should realize that we cannot achieve any healing without faith. Faith is one of the

requirements for receiving any of Gods gifts and blessings. In fact, faith is a basic requirement for making it to heaven. It is just one of the laws that God operates under - and there is no way around it. Love is another one of those mandatory laws and unconditional requirements for salvation. I would have to say that love and faith are the backbone of salvation. You cannot have faith in God without love, and you cannot have true love without faith in God.

Your Faith is the victory that overcomes the world. The world is a system based on selfishness and fear, and Satan is the ruler of this world system. The kingdom of God is based on Love, operates by faith and Jesus is Lord of that Kingdom.**1 John 5:4:** "For whatsoever is born of God, overcomes the world, and this is the victory that overcomes the world, even our Faith."

When pressure and crisis visit, it is your opportunity to develop through faith above its ability to affect you. Your faith is the victory that overcomes the earth.

Here is what the Bible has to say about faith:

Ephesians 2:8 says that we are saved through faith.

Acts 26:18 says that we are sanctified by faith.

Romans 5:1 says that we are justified by faith.

Galatians 2:20 states that we need to live and walk by faith.

Ephesians 6:16 we use the shield of faith to quench all the fiery darts of the wicked one.

Philipians 3:9 our righteousness comes from God by faith.

Collosians 2:7 we are rooted and established in Faith.

Mathew 17:20 faith transforms the impossible to possibilities.

Acts 3:16 says that healing comes through faith.

James 5:15 the prayer of faith saves the sick.

1 John 5:4 our faith is the victory that overcomes and conquers the world.

Romans 14:23 whatever is not of faith is sin.

Hebrews 11:6 It is impossible to please God without faith.

Romans 10:17 " consequently, faith comes from hearing the message, and the message is heard through the word about Christ".

1 Timothy 6:12 teaches us to "fight the good fight of faith; lay hold on the eternal life, where unto though art also called, and has professed a good profession before many witnesses."

Habakab Ch 2:4 "Behold his soul which is lifted up is not upright in him, but the just shall live by faith."

Romans 1:17, "For therein is the righteousness of God, revealed from faith to faith as it is written, the just shall live by faith."

Galatians 3:11 "But that no man is justified by the law in the sight of God is evident, for the just shall live by faith."

Hebrews 10:38 "Now the just shall live by faith…"

Luke 17:5-6 "And the apostles said to the Lord increase our faith, and he said if you have the faith of a grain of mustard seed, you might say to this tree be thy plucked up by the roots and be thus planted in the sea and it should obey you".

Our profession as Christians is our confession of the good word. The "good fight" means a fight that we will win because of our faith! The fight of faith is one of resisting those things that try to move us from what we stand on. We need to stand on the word of God.

The world fears many things; that we will run out of oil, out of gas, out of Food, out of money. But as Christians we have no fear, because we operate on faith. God will take care of us because of our faith. God can cancel our debts, illnesses, and any other problem through our faith. Our faith is our license for reward! Faith cancels all things. Faith needs to be the standard by which we live. We must live in Faith.

Faith is the currency for kingdom results; and it is our ticket to the kingdom. Everything in the kingdom of God operates by faith (such as healing, salvation, blessings). There is only one way to the Father God, and that is through Jesus……..and our faith in this truth shall set us free and will unlock our immortality in the other dimension that awaits God's faithful children.

So how do we live by faith?

We need to read the bible, understand the word. No word - results in - No faith. If our faith level is low it is because our word level is low. Faith is not just about believing, it is acting on what we believe. Clearly knowing what to believe; through knowing the word of God.

You need to plant the seed of faith in your heart, and nourish it with the word, so that it can grow and squeeze out all of doubts out of our mind. If you need some healing, then read the healing scriptures and plant those healing seeds in your mind.

Faith is a practical expression of the confidence that we have in God, and in his word. Faith is conquering all doubts before they become a stronghold in our mind. Real Bible based faith is faith in the Love of God. Faith filled Christians have no doubt about Gods love.

Faith may begin for some when they get a word from God through the Holy Ghost. It will not necessarily be a word that they hear, but they will feel a prodding in their heart, or they may hear it in a dream. But when it happens they will know it. When God spoke to Noah, Abraham, Moses, Samuel, and all of the prophets, they had no doubt that it was the word of God.

But how do we know if these healing manifestations are really from God?

This is one of the excuses that the Pharisees in Jesus day used to have him crucified. They were blinded by Satan into thinking that Satan would actually heal somebody so as to mimic a man of God.

Please remember what I am writing here. Satan would NEVER EVER heal a soul. Satan only wants to afflict and harm us in any way he can. He hates man because he hates God. Since you and I are created in God's image - Satan hates us even the more! His hatred and his jealousy of us are supernatural. He only takes joy in watching us suffer. Nothing good can come from Satan, because he is pure evil. This is why he cannot and will not ever heal a person> After all he is the reason for all illness and suffering in this world!

Indeed, everything evil that happens in this world is influenced by Satan and we can witness it all over the place. When someone hurts us and makes us suffer, remember that behind his actions is Satan. That is why we need to forgive our fellow man.

The bible reveals to us that our battle is not against man, it is against these unseen forces that steals peace from the earth. We

32

read in Ephesians 6:12 "For we do not wrestle against flesh and blood, but against principalities, against powers, against the rulers of the darkness of this age, against spiritual hosts of wickedness in the heavenly places."

Our battle is against the principalities that occupy the heavenly places; the air all around us (includes Satan and demons). This is why Satan is referred as "the prince of the power of the air".

But we can be reassured in knowing that because He who is in you is greater than he who is in the world. (**1 John 4:4**)

Chapter 9 - Closing Comments

John 11:25-26 " Jesus said to her, "I am the resurrection and the life. He who believes in me, though he may die, he shall live. 26 And whoever lives and believes in me shall never die. Do you believe this?"

The world which is presently controlled by Satan pulls us in so many different directions. We are bombarded with life's problems, and it is so easy to lose focus on what really matters - our relationship with the Lord.

We are all distracted by all of the gadgets and pleasures of our time. The computer was designed to make our life easier, but it has just become another form of distraction and a great consumer of time. The media, the social media, economic woes, immorality, geopolitical tension, and…..well, I can go on and on.

The point being, with all the stress that "modern society" imposes upon our mind, body and soul, it's no wonder so many good folks are suffering from one or more forms of illness.

Yet despite all of the noise around us, we can find great peace and joy when we meditate on God's word.

I encourage you to take some time off every day from your busy schedule to seek a quiet place, where you can speak to God and worship his holy name. Tell him what you are feeling this day and ask anything of him. In those quiet moments if you listen real intently, you may just hear his soft gentle voice, providing you with the answer or the solution. During these quiet moments when you are completely focused on the Lord, you will receive that overpowering sense of peace that only our creator can provide.

I pray that this book has provided you with the reassurance that you deserve and desire. In just a few thousand words I have outlined for you the perfect solution for your illness.   So apply it and……..

...Be Healed!

Revelation 21:3-4 "And I heard a loud voice from the throne saying, "Look! God's dwelling place is now among the people and he will dwell with them. They will be his people, and God himself will be with them and be their God. He will wipe every tear from their eyes. There will be no more death' or mourning or crying or pain, for the
old order of things has passed away."

Your fellow servant signs out

Get Complimentary Access to: "Prophecy Alerts"

Dear reader: Prophecies are being fulfilled so rapidly in these last days that I am offering my readers complimentary access to "*prophecy alerts*" so that you get "*Breaking Prophecy News*" as soon as it breaks…Just follow this link below and sign Up today…
http://robertritebooks.com/prophecy-alerts/

About Robert Rite
Robert Rite is the author of over 18 books including:

- "Apocalypse Countdown - 2015 to 2021"
- "Apocalypse Codes - Decoding the Prophecies in the Book of Daniel"

- "100 Proofs that the Bible is the Inspired Word of God and Scientifically Accurate"
- "Ancient Apocalypse Codes"
- "Awaken the Supernatural You!"
- "Aliens, Fallen Angels, Nephilim and the Supernatural"
- "Babylon the Great is Fallen, is Fallen! Who is "Mystery Babylon" of the End of Days?"
- "Blood Moons Rising"
- "Be healed!....How to Unlock the Supernatural Healing Power of God"
- "Bible Verses for Supernatural Blessings"
- End of Days
- "God, Mystery Religions, Cults, and the coming Global Religion"
- "Prophecies of the Apocalypse: Unlocking the End Time Prophetic Codes as Revealed by the Ancient Prophets"
- "Revelation Mysteries Decoded: Unlocking the Secrets of the coming Apocalypse"
- "Signs in the Heavens, Divine Secrets of the Zodiac & the Blood Moons of 2014!"
- "The New Age Movement vs. Christianity: and the Coming Global Religion"
- "Unlocking the Supernatural Power of Prayer"
- "128 Powerful Bible Verses that can Save Your Life!"

   Robert is also the creator of over 135 articles on bible facts, and end-of-day mysteries and prophecies among other related topics. Visit Robert at RobertRiteBooks.com for sample chapters, press releases and related information.

Says Robert Rite:
"It is said that the truth at times is more stimulating than fiction. So have the best of both worlds, and stimulate your mind and soul with subject matter - that really matters"

Robert Rite - Social Profiles:
Blog URLs:
http://RobertRiteBooks.com

Amazon Author Page: http://www.amazon.com/-/e/B00GOGIBEG

Facebook Page: https://www.facebook.com/robertritebooks
Robert Rite at Twitter
Twitter Handle: @robertrite
You Tube Channel:
https://www.youtube.com/channel/UCbED4FN2Pww-u-o1uO0qylQ
Google Plus URL: https://plus.google.com/u/0/100112453810665259776/posts/p/pub
LinkedIn:
https://www.linkedin.com/profile/preview?locale=en_US&trk=prof-0-sb-preview-primary-button
Pinterest: http://www.pinterest.com/frontierins/
Stumble Upon: http://www.stumbleupon.com/stumbler/RobertRite

Instagram: https://instagram.com/robertrite/

www.ingramcontent.com/pod-product-compliance
Lightning Source LLC
Chambersburg PA
CBHW060646030426
42337CB00018B/3480